The Key
to
Wellbeing

Develop a happy
and healthy you

for all your gift books and gift stationery

This edition first published in Great Britain in 2024
by Allsorted Ltd., WD19 4BG.

© Susanna Geoghegan Gift Publishing

Author: Sasha Morton

Illustrator: Jo Parry
Cover and concept design: Jo Parry and Nick Pettit
Contents design: Blackbird Brands

ISBN: 9-781-915902-54-2

Printed in China

10 9 8 7 6 5 4 3 2 1

Introduction

"Wellbeing: The state of being comfortable, healthy, or happy."

Oxford English Dictionary

Everything relating to our sense of wellbeing is connected: from how we feel about our bodies and minds, to whether our finances are secure and if we're satisfied with the social, spiritual and intellectual connections we've made. Each aspect of our wellbeing contributes to the bigger picture of who we are and how we feel about the world we've created for ourselves.

Setting aside time to do what we feel is meaningful or worthwhile often takes a backseat in the hustle and bustle of modern living, but it's important to acknowledge what brings you satisfaction. This book aims to steer you towards better understanding and developing wellbeing skills and strategies that will enhance your day-to-day life.

"The key to a healthy life
is having a healthy mind."

Richard Davidson

"To live a more balanced life,

glance at the past,

live in the present and

focus on the future."

Todd Stocker

Where to begin with wellbeing?

Whether we label it 'wellbeing' or 'wellness', according to the National Wellness Institute, "Wellness is an active process through which people become aware of, and make choices toward, a more successful existence." So where are we meant to start?

Well, there's no one size fits all answer — but solving one part of the wellbeing puzzle often leads to the next piece falling into place. And the progress people make depends on the mindset or circumstances they start from. Ten different people could do the same things and achieve very different outcomes, but nobody will know until they take that first step.

There are different models of what a balanced approach to wellness looks like, with varying numbers of mutually dependent aspects. The aim is to try to maintain a balance in each area in order to live life fully. The following are the principal dimensions of wellness.

- ☀ Emotional

- ☀ Physical

- ☀ Occupational

- ☀ Social

- ☀ Spiritual

- ☀ Intellectual

- ☀ Environmental

- ☀ Financial

"Have faith in your journey. Everything had to happen exactly as it did to get you where you're going next."

Mandy Hale

"NORMAL IS SUBJECTIVE. THERE ARE SEVEN BILLION VERSIONS OF NORMAL ON THIS PLANET."

Matt Haig

Acting your age?

What does the future hold if we are to focus on wellbeing goals as a society? Research shows that different generations have different attitudes towards wellbeing and wellness. Predictions about social trends in wellness suggest that *baby boomers* – usually considered to be people born between the end of World War II and the mid-1960s – who will be hitting their 80s in 2040 – will continue to enjoy a more active retirement lifestyle than their parents' generation.

By 2040, *Generation X* – those born after the baby boomers and before 1980 – will have been exposed to ideas about wellness and work/life throughout their careers, but are predicted to look forward to more relaxing or recuperative activities to undo the damage from any earlier excesses in the 1980s and 1990s!

The *millennial* or *Generation Y* group will be the first generation who have experienced the concept of wellness for their whole lives by 2040. They are most likely to be able to balance meaningful work roles and relationships as they grow older.

Generation Z will be comfortable using social networks and technology to enhance their wellbeing, and will make lifestyle choices based on their existing patterns of behaviour. They are more likely to want to be in charge of shaping the world they live in when they reach their 30s and 40s in 2040 – so watch this space!

"People who can change
and change again are
so much more reliable
and happier than
those who can't."

Stephen Fry

"Life is like riding a bicycle.
To keep your balance you
must keep moving."

Albert Einstein

Habits and routines

Habits and routines are vital to our lives – and are key to our wellbeing. However, it's perfectly natural to feel stuck in a rut sometimes. Some of the things we get on and do because, well, we just need to get on and do them: get up, clean teeth, get dressed, rinse and repeat ad infinitum. Humans fall into repetitive patterns of behaviour because our brains like familiarity. Once a task or routine becomes familiar, the brain uses less energy and does what it needs to do on autopilot. This might have been important for human survival in the Stone Age, but it can sometimes make you feel as though you have a Groundhog Day-style existence rather than a full and varied life.

It can take a minimum of three weeks to form a new habit, such as waking up earlier to go for a quick walk before starting work. If you want to do something to improve your wellbeing, give it time for your goal to become established. Although doing something new feels challenging at first, your brain will eventually create an 'automated response' to process it more easily.

Remember: Anything that helps improve your mental or physical wellbeing is worth taking the time to get right.

"Don't judge each day by the harvest you reap but by the seeds you plant."

Robert Louis Stevenson

"Never give up on what

makes you smile."

Heath Ledger

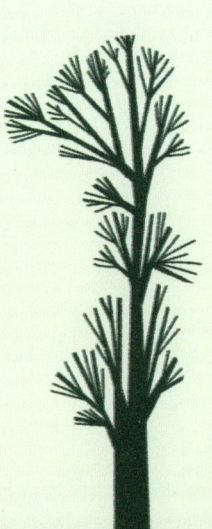

How to form a new habit

Even though the brain enjoys operating within familiar routines, it also likes being rewarded! Whether that's from the success of hitting a fitness target or from a piece of chocolate giving us a sugar rush, anticipation-based activities prompt the brain to release dopamine, also known as the 'feel-good hormone'. The more we get of that, the more of it we want. And once we get used to our brains acknowledging those 'little wins', forming a daily habit should become easier.

Start small

To avoid feeling daunted, take small steps towards your goal. For example, perhaps you want to begin keeping a diary. Rather than thinking you need to write a huge paragraph about your day before bed, start by writing down three words that sum it up. Don't overthink it!

Aim to do this for a for a month, then look back at the body of work you've created – and celebrate it! Repeating small actions and being consistent is the key to forming a new habit that will actually stick.

"Nothing can dim the light which shines from within."

Maya Angelou

"Truth and courage aren't always comfortable, but they're never weaknesses."

Brené Brown

Top tips for setting goals

Improving any aspect of your wellbeing will usually involve setting goals. Here are some tips for making sure you stay on track.

* Only set a goal for something you really want to achieve, whether it's for work or home.

* Make sure your goal is tailored to you, as an individual, not to other people's expectations or demands.

* Be able to summarise your goal in one sentence, for example: 'I am going to work out three times a week.' This is also a more focused target than saying: 'I need to go to the gym more often.'

☀ Break your goal down into smaller, manageable steps.
You might start by doing a weekly fitness class, then
build up to two before reaching your goal of working
out three times a week. These successes are to be
celebrated! Not only will they boost your confidence but
they will release that powerful dopamine as a reward.

☀ Keep track of what you achieve as you work towards
your target, such as recording distances, times or
weights from each exercise session.

Remember: The closer you get to reaching your goal, the
more motivated you'll become.

"WELLNESS ENCOMPASSES A HEALTHY BODY, A SOUND MIND AND A TRANQUIL SPIRIT."

Laurette Gagnon Beaulieu

"To ensure good health:
eat lightly, breathe deeply,
live moderately, cultivate
cheerfulness, and maintain
an interest in life."

William Londen

Healthy body, healthy mind

Incorporating activities into your life each day – either to increase your heart rate or strengthen your muscles – is a sure-fire way to keep your body mobile and your mind focused. You might already do some physical activities as part of your daily routine anyway; if not, by introducing a few of these simple habits into your life, your wellbeing journey will be on the right track.*

Increase your heart rate: Moderate intensity activities
Brisk walking; cycling; water aerobics; hiking; rollerblading; pushing a lawnmower.

Increase your heart rate: Higher intensity activities
Running; swimming; walking up flights of stairs; skipping; aerobics; sports such as football and hockey.

Strengthen your muscles

Yoga; Pilates; Tai Chi; using resistance equipment, bands or your own body weight; carrying heavy shopping bags; heavy gardening, including digging.

* As recommended by www.nhs.uk. Always consult a doctor before starting any new fitness regime if you haven't exercised for a while or have any health concerns.

"He who has health, has hope;
and he who has hope,
has everything."

Arabian proverb

"Everything you do to improve your physical wellbeing will have a positive impact on how good you feel about yourself."

Brian Tracy

Walking for wellbeing

Walking is a great way to be physically active, and among its other benefits, it helps to reduce stress and anxiety. Its wellbeing potential is limitless, especially if you tailor that time to become your own personal therapy session. Whatever you use it for, going out for a walk will always have a physical benefit by releasing mood-boosting endorphins that increase energy, alertness, positivity and self-esteem. Make this your uninterrupted space, away from other distractions. Here are some ideas on how to use it wisely.

☀ Listen to music that you love or challenge yourself to explore new artists or genres.

☀ Spend time with an audiobook or podcast.

✺ Practise 'walking meditation' using an app.

✺ Plan your day.

✺ Talk to a loved one.

✺ Simply allow your mind to wander.

✺ Take photographs of wildlife or scenery you discover.

✺ Turn walking into a new hobby: try Nordic walking, orienteering or geocaching.

✺ Gradually increase your distance or pace to improve your physical fitness.

"You cannot fail

at being yourself."

Wayne W. Dyer

"The best way out

is always through."

Robert Frost

Visible wins!

Once you've decided what you want to achieve to benefit your wellbeing, whether it's getting fitter or being more organised, it can be helpful to deploy some motivational tools or tactics to ensure you stay on track. Try these for size.

- ☀ Set a timer on your smartphone to remind you when to act.

- ☀ Share your goals with people who will reliably act as your support network or cheerleader.

- ☀ Find a goal buddy, and work together to keep each other accountable!

- ☀ Use a calendar, spreadsheet or goal-setting app to track your progress.

☀ Set up a blog to share your wellbeing journey.

☀ Stick a note on your fridge/desk/laptop to remind you of your goal.

☀ Join a group of like-minded individuals with the same aims.

☀ Use wearable tech to keep track of movement, calories, sleep, hydration, and so on.

☀ Keep a goals journal – use pictures and words to keep up your motivation.

☀ Repeat an affirmation, positive statement or quote to lift your spirits if things get tough.

"Always leave enough time in your life to do something that makes you happy, satisfied, even joyous. That has more of an effect on economic wellbeing than any other single factor."

Paul Hawken

"Don't let the noise of others'
opinions drown out your
own inner voice."

Steve Jobs

The power of saying "Yes"!

Being open-minded about doing different things, such as socialising with a new group of friends or trying a different way of working, can bring huge benefits to your mental wellbeing. People who are open-minded tend to find it easier to solve problems, have a more optimistic outlook, are willing to listen to – and learn from – others, and be less judgemental.

The next time someone suggests going somewhere new or even going to see a film in a genre that you wouldn't normally watch, just say, "Yes!" Ask yourself: "What's the worst that could happen?" If you don't enjoy yourself, you don't have to do it again, but at least you gave it a try. And if you have a great experience, you'll feel proud of yourself for having been open-minded enough to participate.

Of course, if you have a genuine reason not to go or take part – because of finances, childcare, travel, logistics, and so on – then don't make things difficult for yourself. Agreeing to do something and then backing out might lead to more stress and anxiety, and a feeling of having let other people down. If you do have to say no, or excuse yourself, always leave things on good terms with the other attendees by wishing them a great time and asking to be invited again.

"Sometimes the people around you won't understand your journey. They don't need to, it's not for them."

Joubert Botha

"REMAIN CALM, BECAUSE PEACE EQUALS POWER."

Joyce Meyer

Let go of the things you can't control

We all like to feel we have control in our lives; it gives us confidence and makes us feel good about ourselves. However, control over some things may not always be within our reach. It might feel hard, but learning not to dwell on things that you can't control – or being less controlling yourself – is one of the kindest things you can do for your wellbeing. There are always things that will happen whether you are concerned about them or not. Sometimes, stepping back and letting a situation unfold without any intervention is the only way to manage it. And while it might be frustrating at the time, once you come to this realisation you will free up valuable headspace and emotional energy.

Write down how different problems make you feel within an hour, a day and a week of them occurring, and see how your own perspective on them changes over time. Could being involved have created a different outcome, or did everything work out anyway?

If you find it hard to give up control, or find yourself repeating controlling behaviours, ask a trusted friend or colleague for support. Let them offer their perspective so that you can start to come up with alternative approaches to issues as they arise. Letting other people see that you trust them to resolve their own problems also builds trust and stronger personal relationships.

"Slow breathing is like an anchor in the midst of an emotional storm: the anchor won't make the storm go away, but it will hold you steady until it passes."

Russ Harris

"We take better care
of our smartphone than
ourselves. We know when
the battery is depleted
and recharge it."

Arianna Huffington

Take a moment to breathe

Your body and mind will thank you for recognising when your wellness batteries are becoming drained. There are days when you might thrive on the adrenaline that comes with achieving your goals. But, at other times, the pace of life can feel overwhelming. Stay on top of a racing mind by taking a moment to breathe.

The technique of 4–4–4–4 breathing will help you to calm your nervous system through increasing the oxygen to your brain, as well as encouraging you to count meditatively. All you need to do is find a comfortable place to sit with your back supported and feet on the floor. When you are ready, follow these steps.

☀ Breathe in through your nose for a count of four.

☀ Hold that breath for a count of four.

☀ Exhale for a count of four.

☀ Wait for four seconds and start again.

Repeat for as long as it takes you to feel relaxed and refocused.

"I am not afraid of storms,

for I am learning how

to sail my ship."

Louisa May Alcott

"Not all storms come to
disrupt your life. Some come
to clear your path."

Paulo Coelho

Life's constant curveballs

"We plan, God laughs."

Yiddish proverb

It's often the case that just when everything feels manageable, life takes an unexpected turn! When upheavals in our personal or professional spheres occur, it's easy to feel overwhelmed at the thought of having to enter the 'crisis management zone'. Here are some tips to help you manage your own wellbeing when times are tough.

🔆 **Get as much sleep as you can:** Try to go to bed and get up at the same time each day. We know that our brains like routine; our bodies do, too.

🌟 **Spend time outdoors every day:** Even if you only manage a quick walk that's okay because standing up, moving around and breathing fresh air generate clarity and focus.

🌟 **Eat well:** Avoid mindless snacking and over-processed foods that can lead to sluggishness and lethargy.

🌟 **Keep hydrated:** Being properly hydrated contributes to better sleep, concentration levels and mood.

🌟 **Reach out:** Ask for practical help, or arrange a regular time to debrief over social media or chat with a trusted person in your life.

"A good laugh and a long sleep are the best cures in the doctor's book."

Irish proverb

"Our bodies are our gardens to which our wills are our gardeners."

William Shakespeare

Our internal emergency cord

When we feel stressed, our sympathetic nervous system gets ready to face whatever danger or challenge our bodies are trying to manage. Muscles become tense, palms get sweaty and our heart rate increases. This is often referred to as the 'fight or flight' response. If we keep pulling on this internal emergency cord, our physical and mental health can suffer.

There are some ways to bring relief to these moments – and for this we need to activate the body's parasympathetic nervous system. This relaxes the body and puts it into a resting and recovery state. The more often we can be in this state, the better it is for our health. Both systems work together to create balance in the body. Here are some useful strategies for stress management to have in your wellbeing toolkit.

☀ Focus on being present in the moment by looking closely at something, listening to the sound of the world around you, holding an object and concentrating on how it feels to the touch.

☀ Ground yourself by placing your bare feet on the earth to restore balance.

☀ Singing or laughing can stimulate the vagus nerve, which is the main nerve in the parasympathetic nervous system. Both these activities also increase oxygen levels in the body, which improves mood and energy.

☀ Practise meditation, or use a meditation app, such as Calm, to reduce stress and increase focus.

"If you keep good food
in your fridge, you will
eat good food."

Errick McAdams

"Healthy living is a combination of mindfulness and action."

Unknown

Get organised!

Eating well contributes to our physical and mental wellbeing, yet it's easy to end up cooking the same few meals on repeat! If this sounds familiar, it's time to break the monotony by getting organised.

Have a clear out

* Bin any foodstuffs that have passed their expiry date. (Dusty jars of herbs and spices are a good place to start!)

* Donate to a foodbank anything within date that you know you won't use.

* Restock store-cupboard basics, such as oils, rice, pasta, tinned tomatoes, stock cubes and condiments. Repeat this process every two or three months.

Start planning

* Encourage everyone in the household to help plan a week of meals, and display your 'menu' so they can see it.

* Keep a list of ingredients alongside the menu so you buy only what you need each week.

☀ Make sure you've bought or defrosted what you need ahead of time each day.

☀ Keep an eye on expiry dates so fresh food doesn't get wasted. Freeze anything you can: this might mean cooking some items first.

☀ Batch cook whatever you can and freeze in single or family-sized portions for later use.

Get inspired

☀ Bookmark recipes from food writers and cooking accounts on social media/online.

☀ Collect recipe cards and free magazines from supermarkets. Cut out the recipes you like and keep them in a book or folder to create your own cookbook.

☀ Borrow recipe books from your library.

☀ Aim to try one new recipe each week!

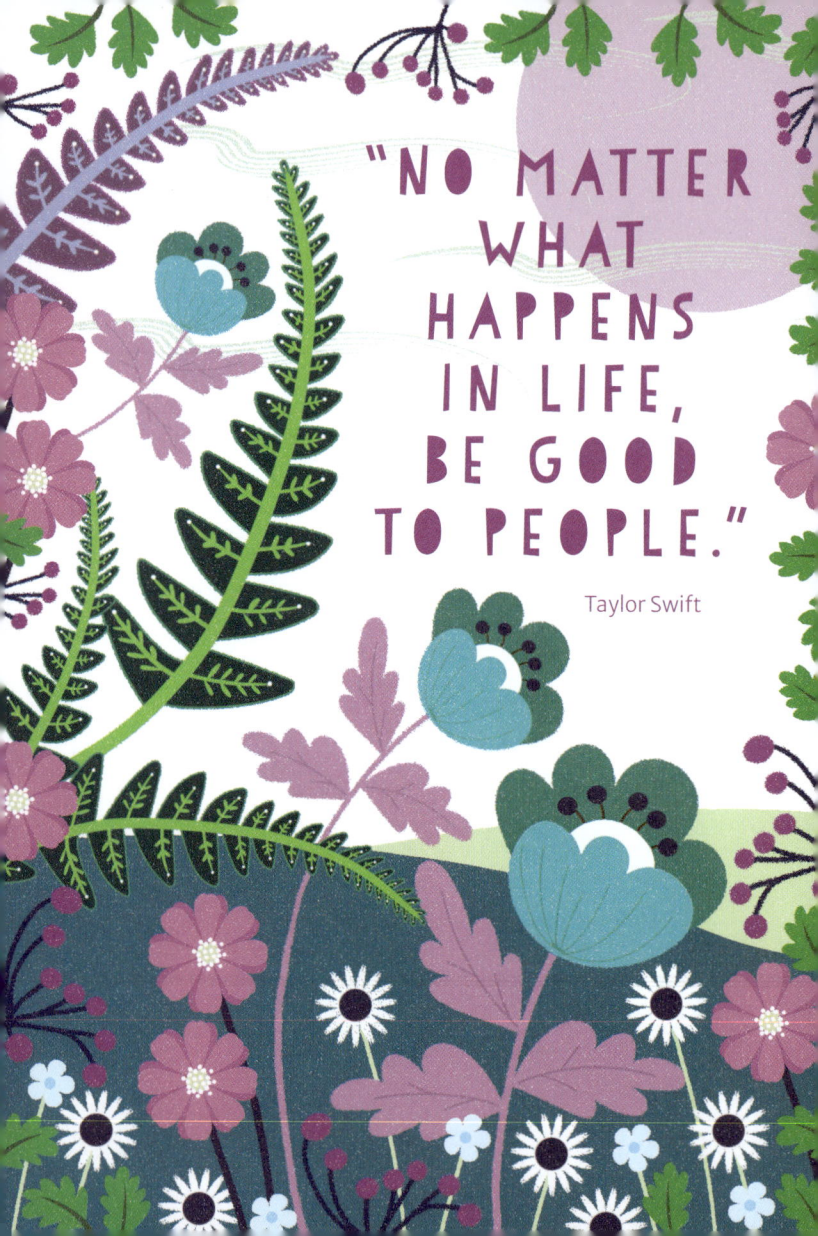

"NO MATTER WHAT HAPPENS IN LIFE, BE GOOD TO PEOPLE."

Taylor Swift

"A healthy attitude is contagious, but don't wait to catch it from others. Be a carrier."

Tom Stoppard

Random acts of kindness

You get what you give in life, and being kind never goes out of fashion. Studies have shown that carrying out acts of kindness are linked to increased feelings of wellbeing, improved mood and relationships, higher levels of self-esteem and a deeper sense of empathy within communities. Even witnessing an act of kindness can do you good by releasing a blood-pressure-reducing, heart-health-increasing chemical called oxytocin, which is known as the 'love hormone'. Doing something for someone else and feeling happier and healthier as a result is a win–win!

If you aren't sure where to start, here are some ideas. Be observant – you're sure to find more ways to help make someone's day!

☀ Let someone with fewer items in their shopping basket ahead of you in the queue.

☀ Donate used towels to animal rescue shelters.

☀ Offer to babysit for a friend or neighbour.

☀ Keep an extra umbrella at work so you can lend it out on a rainy day.

☀ Write a positive online review – these are especially beneficial to small businesses or new authors.

☀ If you receive great customer service, find a manager to let them know who helped you.

"You're only human.
You live once and life is
wonderful, so eat the damned
red velvet cupcake."

Emma Stone

"Overpower.

Overtake.

Overcome."

Serena Williams

You're great – so celebrate!

The next time someone pays you a compliment, instead of making a self-deprecating comment or feeling awkward, hold your head high and accept it with grace. Feelings of self-doubt, or 'imposter syndrome', often rise to the surface when we receive attention at work or within our social circle, but it's okay to celebrate your successes.

By giving yourself permission to accept praise, other people are more likely to notice your appreciation and be pleased that they have made you feel good. Sharing positive news with people also gives them permission to share their own achievements – it's a giving circle, and there's room for everyone! The more we normalise conversations about success, the more likely everyone involved will feel comfortable enough to share and celebrate their own.

"Wellness, I came to realize, will not happen by accident. It must be a daily practice, especially for those of us who are more susceptible to the oppressiveness of the world."

Jenna Wortham

"You can't stop the waves,
but you can learn to surf."

Jon Kabat–Zinn

Practise mindfulness

Practising mindfulness activities can help to replenish energy, reduce stress and relax, which all contribute to better sleep and lower blood pressure. Here are three different mindfulness practices for everyday wellbeing. Try to carve out a time when you can do one or more of these without interruption each day as a dedicated self-care activity.

1. Lie on your back with your arms by your sides with palms facing up, legs extended. Starting with either your head or your toes, focus your attention on each part of your body. Notice any aches, imbalances or sensations, and recognise the thoughts and emotions you associate with each area.

2. Sit with your hands in your lap, feet on the floor and back straight. As you breathe through your nose, concentrate on your breath moving in and out of your body.

If you become distracted, make a mental note of what has interrupted your focus and then return to breathing in and out.

3. Find a space you can quietly spend time in (around 10–20 metres in length is ideal), and slowly walk up and down, or around this area. Take notice of how your steps feel, the tiny adjustments you need to make to maintain your balance, and how your breathing feels as you move.

Give yourself a few moments to breathe, stretch and return your focus to the present at the end of these exercises.

"When I'm not feeling my best I ask myself, 'What are you gonna do about it?'"

Beyoncé

"There are no regrets
in life, just lessons."

Jennifer Aniston

Try something new

As we go through life, we transition through different stages of dressing and personal appearance. Our identities can become tied up in a particular hairstyle or style of clothing, whether we realise it or not. Refreshing our look can remind people that we are individuals with the ability to change and adapt. According to Psychology Today, 'trying something new opens up the possibility for you to enjoy something new'.

A different haircut, a change of colour, trying a beard or removing one ... there's nothing that can't be fixed or grown back in the hair department! Start paying attention to looks and styles that you might not have considered would suit you. Take them along to your next appointment and discuss options with a trusted stylist or barber.

Sort out your clothes and donate or recycle anything you haven't worn for more than two years. Challenge yourself to test out different combinations of clothing so that you select from within your wardrobe rather than buying something new for a couple of months. Take photographs of outfits that are a particular success and make a target list of 'investment items' your wardrobe could benefit from, such as a really good coat or pair of boots.

Most of all, have fun trying out a new you – and remember, life is short, so don't save things for best!

"There is no passion to be
found in playing small
– in settling for a life that
is less than the one you
are capable of living."

Nelson Mandela

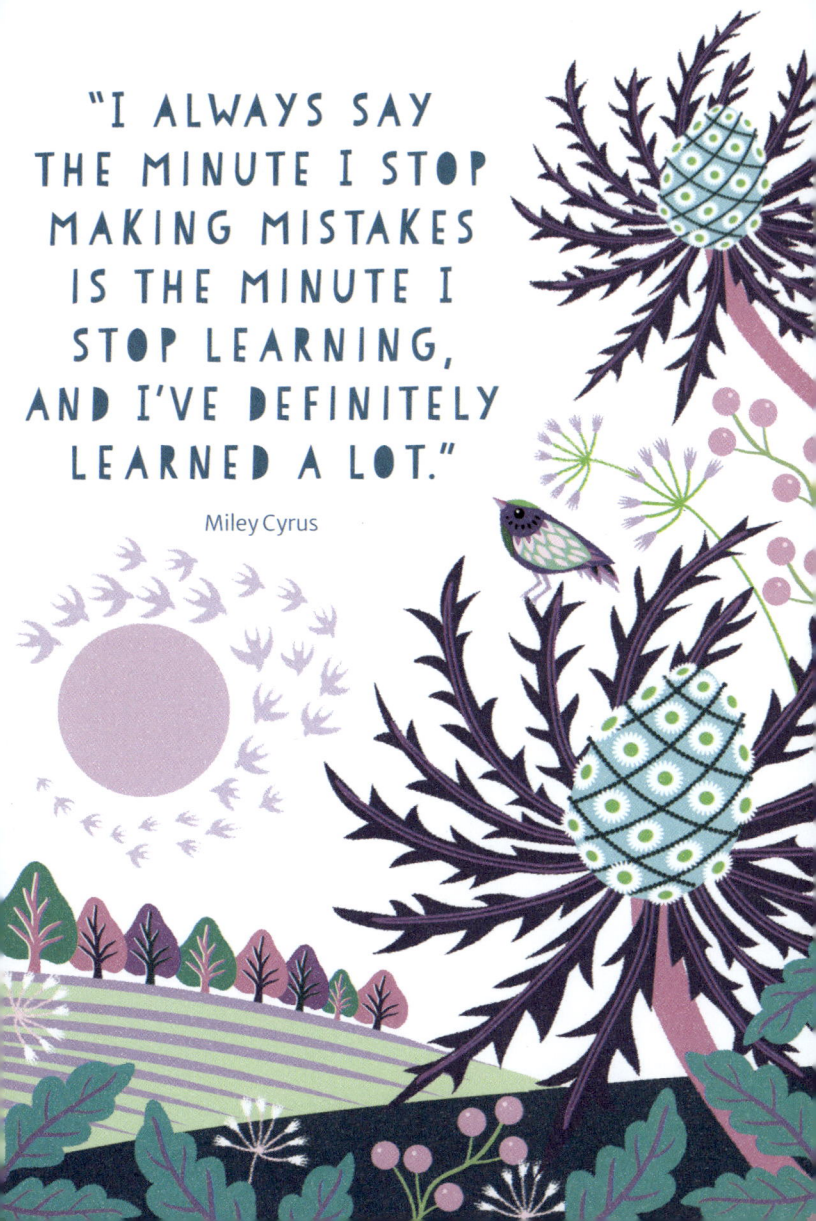

"I ALWAYS SAY
THE MINUTE I STOP
MAKING MISTAKES
IS THE MINUTE I
STOP LEARNING,
AND I'VE DEFINITELY
LEARNED A LOT."

Miley Cyrus

Learn a new skill

Learning something new reminds us that we have the ability to take on new challenges and surprise ourselves. Learning new skills boosts confidence, raises self-esteem and beats boredom, which can only be a good thing. When we try something new, our brains develop new neural pathways, so you'll be encouraging yourself to stay mentally sharp, too!

Whether you pick up something you let drop years ago, or decide to get stuck into a new trend, there's a new skill out there for everyone to benefit from. You might want to try one of these ideas.

☀ Join a book group or running club.

☀ Take up yoga, T'ai Chi or Pilates.

☀ Learn a language.

☀ Learn how to play a musical instrument.

☀ Take a first aid course.

☀ Develop digital literacy skills, such as building apps or websites.

☀ Learn how to make or repair things.

☀ Join a local amateur dramatics production or sing with a choir.

☀ Study for a career change or professional qualification.

☀ Go back to university or college.

"I don't believe in happy
endings, but I do believe
in happy journeys."

George Clooney

"If you're walking down the right path and you're willing to keep walking, eventually you'll make progress."

Barack Obama

Pay attention to the world around you

Various studies have shown that being 'in the moment' can enhance your mood and make you feel more positive about life. Focusing on the present, especially if you are feeling anxious or overwhelmed, helps decrease stress and improves your ability to deal with negative emotions. It also makes you a better listener, increases productivity and improves overall wellness.

Once you have started to focus on being more attentive to how you feel, you may find yourself being more observant to your environment. If you feel like you need a fresher outlook on the places you spend the most time, why not try some of these ideas to give you a new perspective on your usual places and spaces?

* Thoroughly declutter your workstation, around your home or even your car. Donate anything that someone else might benefit from.

* Reorganise an outdoor space to create a sitting area.

* Go somewhere different for lunch and take a walk instead of sitting at your desk or inside.

* Take a different route to or from work, when going for a run or visiting friends.

"I have learned that friendship isn't about who you've known the longest, it's about who came and never left your side."

Yolanda Hadid

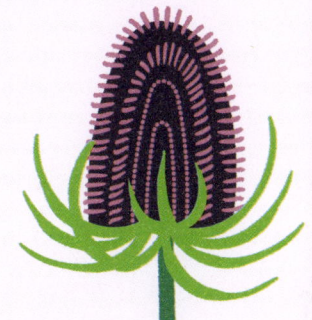

"Whatever you are,

be a good one."

Abraham Lincoln

Friendship goals

Maintaining strong friendships plays a more important role in your ongoing wellbeing than you might think. As well as preventing loneliness and isolation, friendships increase your sense of purpose and self-worth, improve confidence and promote a sense of belonging. Good friends are the people who will celebrate with you, as well as pick you up when you feel down.

Research has shown that adults with strong social connections live longer than those with fewer such connections. They also have a greater sense of support – especially when it comes to dealing with life issues, such as illness, grief and career or family difficulties. They even have a reduced risk of an unhealthy body mass index (BMI), depression and high blood pressure.

Even so, developing and hanging on to new or existing friendships can take time and effort. Like a garden, good friendships need nurturing. To keep friendships flourishing, try to find time to stay in touch, reconnect and reach out. Be the person who picks up the phone even after a long gap in communication – or write a letter to a friend who has been having a tough time. Or, if someone does that for you, be sure to tell them what their friendship means in return.

"What lies behind you and what lies in front of you, pales in comparison to what lies inside of you."

Ralph Waldo Emerson

"'DONE IS BETTER THAN PERFECT.' AIMING FOR PERFECTION CAUSES FRUSTRATION AT BEST AND PARALYSIS AT WORST."

Sheryl Sandberg

Don't be your own worst enemy

While striving for excellence is admirable, there are dangers in trying to aim for perfection in all aspects of your life. It's important to realise that mistakes are inevitable, and being able to handle setbacks shows resilience. From time to time, we will all feel disappointed that we haven't succeeded or met the standard we were hoping for. Learning how to handle this can benefit our wellbeing and reduce the pressure of becoming trapped in a perfectionism cycle. After all, being realistic is never going to make people think less of you!

One useful strategy is to ask a friend to share how they would handle a similar situation. Another is to come up with some positive statements that can reframe your worries and provide a sense of perspective. You might find it helpful to deploy one of these statements if you find yourself feeling self-critical or doubtful over your abilities to deal with different situations, either at home or work.

☀ "Everyone has a bad day – tomorrow I can start again."

☀ "Nobody's perfect!"

☀ "All I can do is my best, and that is enough."

☀ "Everyone makes mistakes – I'm only human."

☀ "I'll ask for help next time."

"... if you do the things
that are easier first, then
you can actually make
a lot of progress."

Mark Zuckerberg

"Always keep your eyes open.

Keep watching.

Because whatever you see

can inspire you."

Grace Coddington

The Pomodoro Technique

In the late 1980s, an Italian university student called Francesco Cirillo began experimenting with different study techniques by using a tomato*-shaped kitchen timer to help him work out the ideal intervals between work and rest. He eventually settled on 25-minute work intervals with a five-minute break between each one. A longer break of 15–30 minutes between every set of four consecutive intervals perfected this time management method.

The Pomodoro Technique (or 'How to get more done and procrastinate less') helps to motivate individuals by steering them towards completing all or part of a longer task in their 25-minute working session, then rewarding them for their progress with that short break before starting again.

Recording progress by noting down what has been achieved during each session is also helpful. So, next time you are struggling to get something crossed off your to-do list, or feel overwhelmed at the thought of starting an activity, perhaps you just need to think tomato …?

> **Top tip: Avoiding distractions during your scheduled 25-minute work time is key: consider turning off social media or keeping your phone on silent (or better still, in a different room).**

*The Italian word for tomato is *pomodoro*.

"Don't spend time beating
on a wall, hoping to
transform it into a door."

Coco Chanel

"The important thing is
to realize that no matter
what people's opinions
may be, they're only just
that – people's opinions.
You have to believe in your
heart what you know to
be true about yourself.
And let that be that."

Mary J. Blige

Managing negative reactions

The way we react to unexpected words, opinions or setbacks can sometimes be hard to control. They trigger the brain to release cortisol, a powerful stress hormone that floods the brain with adrenaline. This primal response would have been great for getting you out of trouble if you were faced with a stampeding woolly mammoth but is less helpful if you've received a snarky comment on social media! Reacting to a sudden shock or upset with tears, sweaty palms, shaking or a racing heart means that pesky combination of hormones is responsible, and your wellbeing can suffer if this becomes a regular occurrence.

When this kind of reaction happens, learning how to convince your brain that everything is okay – so that it can then send out calming chemicals – is necessary. Self-regulation techniques that help manage strong reactions to stressful situations include:

☀ taking a series of calming breaths

☀ counting to five before reacting

☀ physically removing yourself from the situation

☀ taking a short walk

☀ trying to avoid replaying the situation or the way you responded.

Build your resilience for dealing with future flare-ups by practising meditation, being outside in nature and developing creative outlets – all of which help to make stressful situations feel more manageable.

"I really believe you are the company you keep and you have to surround yourself with people who lift you up because the world knocks you down."

Maria Shriver

"Spend time with people
who know how to use
their days well."

Rihanna

Find good role models

Looking up to someone, and admiring what they have achieved, can provide inspiration, motivation and support, whether they're a family member, friend, colleague, expert, creator or celebrity. Role models can help us feel a sense of purpose – that hitting goals is possible and that obstacles can be overcome. Positivity often comes from seeing others succeed, and role models can help us see the potential in ourselves that we might otherwise overlook.

Here are some questions to ask if you are trying to find a role model of your own.

✸ Do their beliefs and values align with your own?

✸ Do you feel their words or actions would be helpful during difficult times?

☀ Do they operate within a field that you already work in, or would like to?

☀ Do they openly share how they have achieved their successes?

Strong female role models
Michelle Obama, Greta Thunberg, Malala Yousafzai, Ruth Bader Ginsburg, Taylor Swift.

Strong male role models
Dwayne Johnson, Trevor Noah, Sir David Attenborough, Denzel Washington, Harry Styles.

"FRIENDSHIP IS BORN AT THE MOMENT WHEN ONE MAN SAYS TO ANOTHER, 'WHAT! YOU TOO?'"

C.S. Lewis

"Find a group of people who challenge and inspire you; spend a lot of time with them, and it will change your life."

Amy Poehler

Meet new people

While a degree of solitude can actually promote wellness, loneliness and feelings of isolation can lead to poor mental health. Loneliness is something that significant numbers of people suffer from in the 21st century. Interacting regularly with people – even for a few hours – gives structure to our time, builds a sense of belonging and boosts our wellbeing. Even if we have a fabulous group of friends, we can find ourselves growing bored of the same conversations or experiences.

Expanding your social circle can be exhilarating and nerve-wracking all at the same time. One of the best ways to establish new relationships is to look for common ground. A shared appreciation of a particular hobby or activity creates natural conversational topics, and thanks to social media, connecting to people with similar interests has never been easier. You could even set up your own group!

Here are some ideas for meeting new people.

- ☀ Join a supporters' group for your favourite sports team.

- ☀ Find a local book group or book chat forum on social media and sign up to some shared reading challenges.

- ☀ Enrol on a course or class.

- ☀ Volunteer! Donate your time to a charity shop, retirement home or foodbank.

- ☀ Go on a park run or join a walking/hiking club.

- ☀ Join a gym and book some classes or training sessions.

- ☀ Chat to people when you're walking your dog.

- ☀ Participate in community forums and neighbourhood groups.

"We pass through this

world but once."

Stephen Jay Gould

"… one can remain alive …
if one is unafraid of change,
insatiable in intellectual
curiosity, interested in
big things, and happy
in small ways."

Edith Wharton

Experience culture in real life

Feeling stuck in a cultural rut? With a constant supply of streaming channels and information beamed onto our screens 24/7, it can almost feel as if there's no need to leave home – but you can't beat the feeling of being immersed in a cultural experience in real life. It's a great way to boost your wellness: you'll feel more alert, engaged with the outside world and motivated to take part yourself – or share what you've seen and heard with other people. Look out for these enriching cultural opportunities: most are promoted online and can be found all over the country.

Concerts: From candlelit concerts in churches, to pub bands and massive stadium gigs, there's nothing like being part of a crowd living in the musical moment.

Galleries: As well as permanent exhibits, most museums and art galleries have pop-up or featured shows, workshops or special events so you can dip your toe in the water of something new.

- **Live performances:** If you can't get to a theatre, or the ticket price is too high, many cinemas now stream live performances of musicals, plays, opera, comedy or dance that are just as good as the real thing!

- **Farmers' markets and food festivals:** These are a great opportunity to support local community endeavours, pop-up stalls and small or artisanal producers.

- **Cultural festivals:** Experience different cultures, clothing, food, music, entertainment and arts.

"Nothing in life is to be feared,
it is only to be understood.
Now is the time to understand
more, so that we may fear less."

Marie Curie

"Life shrinks or expands in

proportion to one's courage."

Anaïs Nin

Be spontaneous

"Spontaneous: Performed as a result of a sudden impulse or inclination; having an open, natural and uninhibited manner."

Oxford English Dictionary

Not everyone is naturally spontaneous — but it can be a remarkably useful characteristic to try to develop. People who have a spontaneous nature tend to have a positive outlook and are comfortable and secure enough in themselves to act on their instincts. They worry less, and are more creative and flexible. This leads to an increased sense of happiness and a greater ability to deal with stress because they find ways to relieve pressure points before they intensify.

Being spontaneous can mean different things to different people: there are no rules for spontaneity. If you struggle to live spontaneously, start by doing one small, unplanned thing, such as going for a quick walk after dinner, or setting off for a drive or cycle with no set destination in mind. Order a takeaway from a different place. Invite someone over. Play a board game!

Spontaneous people take advantage of opportunities that present themselves, they are adaptable and don't dwell on things that change. While being organised and planning ahead has its place, in some situations it can be exciting to live in the moment and go with the flow— so why not try to bring some spontaneity into your life?

"Play to your strengths. If you aren't great at something, do more of what you're great at."

Jason Lemkin

"The secret of change is to focus all of your energy not on fighting the old, but on building the new."

Socrates

Ask yourself why

Setting professional goals is a great way to move forwards at work, but the key to successful career development is as much about thinking why you're doing something, as well as how you'll get there. Asking yourself why you want to achieve something is the energy source that will power your future personal development. For example:

※ Do you want to feel acknowledged, drive change or have a positive impact on the people around you?

※ What part of your professional life brings you the most satisfaction?

※ Can you get feedback from other people to identify areas of strength and weakness you may not be aware of?

☀ Do you have colleagues and contacts you can talk to about their passions and aspirations?

☀ Can you find a way to make your personal values align to your work goals?

By working out why you are setting these goals, you'll have a greater sense of purpose and be motivated to apply this form of questioning to other aspects of your life for greater wellbeing satisfaction.

"Because when you are imagining, you might as well imagine something worth while."

L.M. Montgomery

"THINK AND WONDER. WONDER AND THINK."

Dr Seuss

Power of daydreaming

Contrary to what your teachers may have told you if you were caught gazing out of the window at school, daydreaming is not a bad habit that you need to break. There are many benefits to having the capacity to daydream in your wellness toolkit.

Research has shown that people who can let their mind wander experience less stress; allowing our thoughts to flow freely helps our brains to relax. This is crucial for our productivity and energy as our brains can't maintain focus without some downtime.

Daydreaming – as a response to rising anxiety or stressful situations – can help bring overwhelming feelings under control. If you start to feel your heart racing or your breathing becoming shallow, stop what you are doing; look away from your computer or work; take a deep breath; and allow yourself to think of something that brings you happiness or a positive memory.

The same research has also shown that those who daydream are:

- ☀ better problem-solvers

- ☀ more likely to achieve their goals

- ☀ more creative

- ☀ forging stronger connections between different parts of the brain.

"Balance is not something
you find, it's something
you create."

Jana Kingsford

"Music can change
the world because it
can change people."

Bono

The magic of music

Music has long been accepted as a form of therapy to improve people's mental health and quality of life. There's nothing like hearing a special song to take you back to a particular time or place, or dancing to a much-loved tune to provide a natural high – even hearing 15 minutes of music can make you feel happier. You can feel the wellness benefits yourself by introducing some of these scientifically proven habits into your daily routine.

* **Listening to relaxing classical music** for 45 minutes before bed helps promote better-quality sleep and reduces insomnia.

* **Listening to music while driving** can have a positive impact on mood, leading to safer behaviour on the roads.

☀ **Listening to relaxing music before surgery** decreases anxiety and can even reduce the need for medication to help patients feel relaxed.

☀ **Taking music lessons can improve academic performance** and verbal fluency in young children, so encourage them to pick up an instrument or sing!

☀ **Participating in a musical performance** can have an even more positive effect than just listening to music (which, in itself, reduces stress) by decreasing the level of cortisol in our bodies.

☀ **Listening to motivational music** while running improves performance.

"Work is a rubber ball. If you drop it, it will bounce back. The other four balls – family, health, friends, integrity – are made of glass. If you drop one of these, it will be irrevocably scuffed, nicked, perhaps even shattered."

Gary Keller

"We need to do a
better job of putting
ourselves higher on
our own 'to-do' list."

Michelle Obama

Just say "No"

As well as being open to saying yes, sometimes the best thing you can do for yourself is to say no. Most of us are guilty of agreeing to do things we don't have time for, don't want to do, or feel obligated to take on. We feel guilty about letting people down or appearing unhelpful. However, to achieve balance in your life and to benefit your mental health and wellbeing, there's no harm in making other people aware that you are setting boundaries for yourself. Here are some useful phrases to use when you need to let yourself off the hook (politely) and protect yourself from feeling overwhelmed!

* "I'm sorry, this isn't a good time."

* "I'd love to, but I can't."

- ☀ "I'm not actually taking on anything new at the moment."

- ☀ "Thanks for thinking of me, but I won't be able to fit it in."

- ☀ "Let me get back to you, but it's probably not going to be possible."

- ☀ "I'm afraid I can't, but I appreciate being asked."

- ☀ "Under different circumstances that would have been great, but I'll have to pass for now."

"Life isn't about finding yourself. Life is about creating yourself."

George Bernard Shaw

"Don't get so busy making

a living that you forget

to make a life."

Dolly Parton

Me time

You may have heard the expression 'me time' and felt sceptical about needing to put a title on something as simple as allocating time to yourself. However, it can be a useful way of carving out a slot just for you to spend as you wish. Treat it as a scheduled wellness activity in much the same way that you might put a doctor's appointment or an exercise class in your diary. Use it as an opportunity to try something new, go somewhere solo, or just have a restorative afternoon nap.

Scientifically speaking, having some personal time benefits our wellbeing in a range of different ways.

☀ It forces us to invest in ourselves and prioritise our own satisfaction.

☀ It's an opportunity to focus on our own wellbeing and happiness.

☀ Time alone lets our brains reboot, improving concentration and making us more productive.

☀ We become more patient and engaged with other people afterwards.

☀ It gives us something to plan for, and look forward to.

☀ It can allow time for self–discovery and deeper thinking.

☀ It resets and restores our physical and mental energy so that we can take on challenges.

"If they can make penicillin out of mouldy bread, they can sure make something out of you."

Muhammad Ali

"How wonderful it is that nobody need wait a single moment before starting to improve the world."

Anne Frank

(Don't) read all about it

Staying up to date with what is happening in the world has many benefits; it enables us to understand what is going on around us, exposes us to different perspectives and promotes cross-cultural understanding. However, gathering knowledge about issues that concern us can be a balancing act. There's a fine line between finding out helpful information and convincing yourself that the end of the world is nigh. For your own wellbeing, there are steps you can take to avoid stress and anxiety and to protect your mental health at the same time.

The 24/7/365 news cycle can have an impact on people's wellbeing because of regular exposure to negative or distressing events. If hearing, watching or reading news reports is making you feel depressed or fearful for the future, don't be afraid to switch it off. Trust that any noteworthy events or developments will reach you.

Thanks to the proliferation of online forums, websites and the unreliable vetting of credible sources on social media, misinformation is rife in today's world. Whatever your information source, employing critical thinking to consider whether you are being guided towards a particular perspective will help you to assess the motive of the writer or broadcaster. Use reliable, non-partisan sources and read widely around a topic of particular interest so that you gain a broader range of viewpoints.

"Sometimes, carrying on,
just carrying on, is the
superhuman achievement."

Albert Camus

"... decide ... whether or
not the goal is worth
the risks involved.
If it is, stop worrying ..."

Amelia Earhart

Quiet quitting

During 2022, the concept of 'quiet quitting' went viral on social media apps. It summarised a shift in workplace attitudes towards fulfilling only core job requirements and not taking on additional responsibilities, using initiative or working overtime. Post-pandemic, some in the workforce struggled to engage with work in the way they had before. For many, this was about conserving their mental and physical wellbeing; for others, it was the outcome of realising they may have been placing too much energy on what their employers wanted, to the detriment of their own work–life balance.

This reduced inclination to engage with work and workplace cultures created concern over employees' wellbeing and the lack of boundaries between their work and personal lives. Some companies have since committed to re-establishing stronger boundaries so that employees aren't expected to complete work or to attend meetings/training/social events outside their contracted work times.

If this resonates with how you feel about work, or if you feel that you are fast approaching burnout, make an appointment to speak with your manager or HR department. Ask your employer to take the time to listen to your concerns and come up with a solution that rewards both sides.

"It is time for us all to stand and cheer the doer, the achiever – the one who recognizes the challenges and does something about it."

Vince Lombardi

"I might not be the brightest
bulb in the chandelier,
but I'm pretty good at
getting most of the other
bulbs to light up."

Jack Welch

Get involved

You might be driven to despair by potholes or feel as though you're on the back foot over bin collections. Whatever your frustration about the way your local area is managed, there's every possibility your local council or government will appreciate volunteers who can identify issues and make things better. People with good communication skills who have retired or are on a career break are the perfect candidates. So, if you think you could make a difference – and improve other people's quality of life as well as your own – why not do one of these activities?

* Attend a local community, town planning or village/town hall meeting.

* Participate in fundraising events for community projects.

* Organise litter-picking or beach/countryside clean-ups.

* Volunteer to help a political party or campaign.

✴ Raise awareness of issues with local newspapers/online media.

✴ Sign petitions and offer to collect signatures for causes you believe need attention.

✴ Become a local councillor or neighbourhood coordinator.

✴ Contribute to discussions about local issues on online forums and help groups.

✴ Become a school governor.

"The scariest moment
is always just
before you start."

Stephen King

"If you spend too much time thinking about a thing, you'll never get it done."

Bruce Lee

Feel the fear and do it anyway

Everyday pressures can lead to paralysis. Here are some tips for dealing with the most common ones that can have an impact on our wellness.

❋ If personal health issues are occupying your mind, always make an appointment with a medical professional to put your mind at rest or find a way to resolve them. It's too easy to focus on negative outcomes based on online assessments or conversations with friends and family and miss actual problems.

❋ Putting off life admin that has a financial impact, such as your annual tax return or insurance renewals, is understandable. Set aside a time when you have no other distractions to get any paperwork in order first, then make sure you know any passwords you might need. Turn off social media, put a 'Do not disturb' sign on yourself if you need to, and get started! The thought of these activities is typically worse than doing them – and you'll feel a great sense of relief and satisfaction afterwards. Plan a reward for when you've either got the process started or completed, such as going out with friends or relaxing with a book and a cup of tea!

* If you feel guilty over being late in replying to friends' texts, emails or social media posts, or need to resolve a personal conflict or family issue, take a deep breath and just reach out. There are very few things that are worse than silence.

"IF YOU
ALWAYS DO
WHAT INTERESTS
YOU, AT LEAST
ONE PERSON
IS PLEASED."

Katharine Hepburn

"Keeping busy and making
optimism a way of life
can restore your faith
in yourself."

Lucille Ball

Kickstart creativity

Children are encouraged to be creative, but as we grow into adulthood, these kinds of pastimes often fall by the wayside. Expressing ourselves creatively can improve mood, concentration and feelings of self-esteem and confidence. Being creative is proven to alleviate loneliness and boredom, make us more resourceful and provide a sense of purpose.

Hobbies can be more than just ways to occupy our time. When we become focused on one specific creative task, we enter what is called a state of 'flow' – which means we are so absorbed in what we are doing, we stop letting negative thoughts cloud our minds. Some hobbies make us more sociable because we can do them with a partner or small group, such as singing or gardening. Other hobbies, such as playing a musical instrument, writing or or journaling, can increase our cognitive function by activating different parts of the brain.

To kickstart your creativity, start with a small project to see what suits you – colouring, doodling or sketching, jigsaw puzzles, knitting or crochet, baking, gardening, model-making, photography, keeping a scrapbook. One hobby may well lead to another – you've nothing to lose and everything to gain!

"Alone we can do so little;

together we can do so much."

Helen Keller

"Every person is defined by the communities she belongs to."

Orson Scott Card

Giving back

Helping others through volunteering, or taking on extra responsibilities within your family or local community, is hugely beneficial to the recipients, but volunteering also provides rewards for those who take part; it increases feelings of wellbeing, self-esteem and social connection. Participating in, or running, events to support others means putting someone before yourself, so it's important to make sure you have the bandwidth to do this before committing.

Small starter steps towards giving back could include simple tasks you can build into your own day, such as helping a neighbour or elderly friend or relative by walking their dog, dropping off shopping, helping with light household chores or posting letters or parcels.

Volunteers are also appreciated in childcare or educational settings, for example, in helping with reading practice, assisting with lunch and breaktime support, sharing a skill, such as cooking, computing or arts and crafts. Care homes often welcome volunteers who can sit with residents to play games, do puzzles or just provide companionship.

Make your willingness or availability known to people or online volunteer groups – and see what opportunities come your way!

"Appreciation is a wonderful thing: It makes what is excellent in others belong to us as well."

Voltaire

"Mutual respect is the foundation of genuine harmony."

Dalai Lama

Surprise!

Feeling appreciated or noticed drives people to do their best and forges empathy and a sense of connection. Yet all too often we feel awkward or uncomfortable offering unsolicited praise or telling people that we are grateful to have them in our lives.

One of the nicest things we can do for someone is to surprise them by telling or showing them how much we respect, admire and care for them. If you have a sense that someone has been going through a tough time, even if they don't say so, it never hurts to send them a quick message or call them to check in. If there's a reason to celebrate their successes, let them know that you feel proud of them – and toot their horn to other people to share the good news.

Writing a letter or sending a card is a lovely thing to do – and to receive. Acting spontaneously, without overthinking these kinds of gestures, can become habit-forming and rekindle relationships that may otherwise go on the back burner because of our busy lives, which is another wellness win!

"Never apologize for
trusting your intuition
– your brain can play tricks,
your heart can be blind,
but your gut is always right."

Rachel Wolchin

"YOUR INNER VOICE, YOUR INSTINCT, KNOWS EVERYTHING."

Henry Winkler

Follow your instincts

"Intuition: The ability to understand something instinctively, without the need for conscious reasoning."

Oxford English Dictionary

Acting intuitively, listening to your gut, following your instincts – all of these are ways to describe how we sometimes just 'know' the right way to proceed, without relying on deeper thought. Being able to act instinctively can sometimes involve a substantial leap of faith, but in doing so, you're proving that you can commit to something on the basis of self-belief.

The opposite of intuition is overthinking; this is something of which many of us are guilty. Overthinking can lead to paralysis and catastrophising, working through multiple worst-case scenarios and getting nowhere. There's a balance to be had between instinct and overthinking that will enable you to make decisions and move on in confidence – but it takes practice to deliver the best outcome for your wellbeing. One middle-ground solution is to write down a problem, situation or issue and what you think you should do about it. Then distract yourself for 24 hours and see if circumstances or your perspective change. Sometimes, just the act of writing down a problem, or an anxious thought, can be enough to resolve how you feel about it. If you are left feeling convinced your instincts are correct, you know you are on the right path.

"Being rich is having money;
being wealthy is having time."

Margaret Bonnano

"It is better to look ahead and prepare than to look back and regret."

Jackie Joyner-Kersee

Financial wellness

There's nothing worse than dreading the arrival of a bank statement or fearing you've exhausted your overdraft limit. If you find yourself holding your breath when you hand over your debit or credit card, it's time to make putting your finances in order a priority. Financial wellness is a long game, but these tips should help you turn a corner sooner.

🌸 **Record your outgoings:** Keep a spreadsheet or use an app to record all of your outgoings. Use what you learn about your spending habits to make changes.

🌸 **Set a budget:** Be realistic and set goals that are going to be manageable.

🌸 **Start a savings account:** Once you see what you have left at the end of the month, organise an automatic transfer into a savings account as soon as you get paid – and aim to accrue at least three months' salary in savings.

 **Paying off debt:** If you can't pay off any credit or store card expenditure in full each month, transfer outstanding balances to a credit card with a lower interest rate. Always pay off the card with the highest interest rate first.

"You should sit in meditation
for 20 minutes a day,
unless you're too busy.
Then you should sit
for an hour."

Zen saying

"Never waste any amount of time doing anything important when there is a sunset outside that you should be sitting under!"

C. JoyBell C.

Gratitude journal

Gratitude journals can help people increase their sense of wellness by making them consider all the positive aspects of their lives. Appreciating all the things we have makes us more optimistic. It gives us a way to process envy, frustration, regret and other negative thoughts and emotions, and it promotes self-esteem and confidence.

From a health perspective, pausing to feel thankful activates the parasympathetic nervous system (the system that helps us to digest and rest), which can reduce blood pressure, heart rate and breathing. Each of these benefits contribute towards feeling more relaxed and in control. So, where should you start?

☀ **Ready-made gratitude journals:** These have fill-in sections and prompts (such as: Today, I am grateful for ...; I'm proud of ...; Tomorrow, I look forward to ...; Today, I let go of ...) and space to write down thoughts, feelings and affirmations.

☀ **Gratitude jar:** Write down something you are grateful for on a slip of paper and pop it in a dedicated jar or box each day. Reread them when you need a mood boost!

☀ **Record a daily moment of gratitude in your diary.**

"I took a walk in the woods
and came out taller
than the trees."

Henry David Thoreau

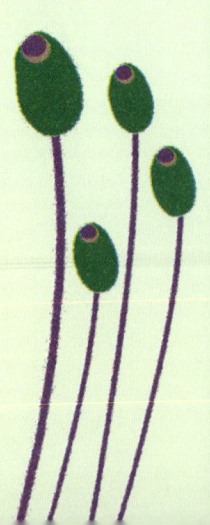

"Being able to smell the fresh air and disconnect from the news and your phone – there's nothing like it."

Jason Ward

Get back to nature

In recent years, studies from around the world have found that there are significant wellbeing benefits to be gained from spending time in nature. These range from the mental – reducing feelings of anger and stress; becoming more sociable and relaxed – to the physical – promoting cardiovascular health; improving fitness; reducing muscle tension and the risk of disease. The lists go on, but the fact remains: there are so many upsides to getting outdoors, why wouldn't you?

It's time to stop making excuses and get motivated! Here are some things to consider so that you can find a way to make being outside suit your lifestyle.

☀ Being outside for around 120 minutes per week, either in one visit or split across different outings, is optimal.

☀ Consider whether you could move your workout outdoors.

☀ Make it a scheduled activity with a friend, walking group or family members.

☀ If you're going outside alone, make sure you're in a space where you feel safe.

☀ Don't get distracted by your phone or use the time to combine work and movement – be fully in the moment.

☀ Practise mindful breathing and listen to the sounds around you.

"If you truly love
nature, you will find
beauty everywhere."

Vincent van Gogh

"Over every mountain
there is a path, although
it may not be seen
from the valley."

Theodore Roethke

Reconnect

In busy times, or just in day-to-day life, we can forget who is important to us, or take people for granted. Our loved ones are our wellness anchor. They are the people who accept us for who we are, regardless of our faults and flaws. When we are distracted by other tasks, losing sight of how much they mean to us can create a disconnect. Here are some strategies to restore these vital connections.

- **Pay attention:** Listen to what your loved ones are saying and take notice of the things going on in their lives. Pay special attention to any changes in behaviour and address these before they turn into deeper issues.

- **Have a digital detox:** Spend time with each other in real life, start conversations, pay each other compliments and do things together that don't involve social media or technology.

☀ **Broaden your experiences:** Take up a new hobby together, have a regular date night, join a club or society, make dinner together, see friends more often.

☀ **Prioritise regular family time:** Make a meal together, play a board game, go for a walk or plan a trip.

☀ **Say, "I love you!"**

"Red flags are the
universe's way of saying,
'Pause, reflect and reassess.'"

Dee Waldeck

"The human instinct
for self-preservation
is strong."

Nancy Werlin

Power nap o'clock

"Power nap: A short sleep taken during the working day in order to restore one's mental alertness."

Oxford English Dictionary

Fatigue, tiredness, exhaustion … all of these can have an impact on our physical and mental wellbeing, leading to loss of concentration, poor memory function and low mood. There are no prizes for existing on limited amounts of sleep – our bodies and minds need it as much as they need food, water and sunlight. The solution? Taking a short power nap!

Having a short snooze can have huge benefits, including improved focus and memory, and reduced stress. According to www.sleepfoundation.org, this is the best way to do it so that you come out feeling refreshed on the other side!

☀ Set an alarm for anywhere between 15 and 30 minutes (any longer and you'll feel sluggish when you wake up).

☀ Lie down comfortably in a cool room.

☀ Turn off or activate silent/airplane mode on any devices.

☀ Switch off all light sources and use an eye mask or use blackout blinds/thick curtains to block out light.

☀ Insert earplugs.

☀ Clear your mind and sleep.

☀ Hydrate when you wake up.

☀ Get some fresh air if you feel any residual tiredness.

"Find out who you are
and do it on purpose."

Dolly Parton

"Don't take life too seriously.

You will never get out of it alive."

Elbert Hubbard

Wise words for wellness

Love deeply.

Live authentically.

Learn wholeheartedly.

Participate enthusiastically.

Laugh loudly.

Celebrate happily.

Decide wisely.

Think intuitively.

Share unquestioningly.

Donate meaningfully.

Forgive gracefully.

Speak thoughtfully.

Praise generously.

Listen carefully.

Act kindly.

Eat healthily.

Sleep deeply.

"Who you are is

beautiful and amazing."

Laverne Cox